The Sinking of the *Lusitania*: The Most Controversial Submarine Attack of World War I

By Charles River Editors

The Lusitania

About Charles River Editors

Charles River Editors provides superior editing and original writing services across the digital publishing industry, with the expertise to create digital content for publishers across a vast range of subject matter. In addition to providing original digital content for third party publishers, we also republish civilization's greatest literary works, bringing them to new generations of readers via ebooks.

Sign up here to receive updates about free books as we publish them, **and visit** Our Kindle Author Page **to browse today's free promotions and our most recently published Kindle titles.**

Introduction

A 1915 painting depicting the sinking of the *Lusitania*

The Sinking of the *Lusitania*

"The sounds of that awe-inspiring requiem that vibrated o'er the ocean have been drowned in the waters of the deep, the instruments that gave them birth are silenced as the harps were silenced on the willow tree, but if the melody that was rehearsed could only reverberate through this land 'Nearer, My God, to Thee,' and its echoes could be heard in these halls of legislation, and at every place where our rulers and representatives pass judgment and enact and administer laws, and at every home and fireside, from the mansions of the rich to the huts and hovels of the poor, and if we could be made to feel that there is a divine law of obedience and of adjustment, and of compensation that should demand our allegiance, far above the laws that we formulate in this presence, then, from the gloom of these fearful hours we shall pass into the dawn of a higher service and of a better day, and then, Mr. President, the lives that went down upon this fated night did not go down in vain." – Senator Isidor Rayner

In 1906, the RMS *Lusitania* was at the forefront of transatlantic shipping. Briefly the largest ship in the world, the designers and engineers who built the *Lusitania* aimed for her to represent the height of luxury for passengers while also being the harbinger of a new technological age, replete with revolutionary engines that would allow the gigantic ship to move at speeds that would have been considered impossible just years earlier. Indeed, the highly competitive industry would spur the development of bigger and better ocean liners in the coming years, the most famous being the *Titanic*.

The *Lusitania* and the *Titanic* would become the two most famous ships of the early 20th century for tragic reasons, but the circumstances could not have been more different. While the *Titanic* is still notorious for being the world's best ocean liner at the time of its collision with an iceberg in 1912, the *Lusitania*'s role as a popular ocean liner has been almost completely obscured by the nature of its sinking by a German U-boat in 1915. The Germans aimed to disrupt trade by the Allied forces, but they did not have the naval forces capable of seizing merchant ships and detaining them. Furthermore, the Germans rightly suspected that the British and Americans were using passenger liners and merchant ships to smuggle weaponry across the Atlantic, but since their sole edge in the Atlantic was their fleet of submarines, the Germans had no way of confirming their suspicions, short of sinking a ship and seeing if a detonation onboard suggested the presence of munitions and gunpowder.

The Germans targeted many British merchant ships, but on May 7, 1915, a German U-boat controversially torpedoed the *Lusitania*, which sank less than 20 minutes after being struck. The attack killed over 1,000 people, including over 100 American civilians, infuriating the United States. After sinking the ship, the Germans immediately claimed that the boat was carrying "contraband of war" and was in a war zone, charges vehemently denied by the United States and the British. For awhile, the Germans tightened restrictions on their use of U-boats to placate the Americans and seek to keep them out of the war (though the restrictions would not last).

The sinking of the Lusitania in 1915 was the first major event that shifted public opinion in the United States, and support for joining the war began to rise across the country. Many Americans joined the "Preparedness Movement," which advocated at least preparing for war if not entering the war outright, and though the country would not declare war against Germany for two more years, the sinking of the *Lusitania* is still cited as a key event that set America on the path toward joining the war.

Given the importance of its sinking, debate over whether the *Lusitania* was carrying explosive munitions has raged on ever since. When the U-boat's torpedo hit the *Lusitania* and exploded, a second explosion followed the first explosion shortly after, and the Germans cited the second explosion as evidence that the torpedo had hit weapons munitions that ignited the second explosion, a charge that was strongly denied by the British. It would take multiple investigations, declassified documents, and even dives to the wreckage to determine whether the *Lusitania* was smuggling arms, and whether such munitions triggered the second explosion.

The Sinking of the Lusitania chronicles the construction and destruction of one of the most notorious ships of the 20th century. Along with pictures of important people, places, and events, you will learn about the sinking of the *Lusitania* like never before, in no time at all.

The Sinking of the *Lusitania*: The Most Controversial Submarine Attack of World War I
About Charles River Editors
Introduction
   Chapter 1: The Largest Ship in the World
   Chapter 2: The Start of World War I
   Chapter 3: Bound for Liverpool
   Chapter 4: "A Million-Ton Hammer"
   Chapter 5: Abandoning Ship
   Chapter 6: Total Loss
   Chapter 7: Certain Statements
   Bibliography

Chapter 1: The Largest Ship in the World

The *Lusitania* before it was launched

"The ship was built of steel by John Brown and Company, at Clydebank, in 1907. She had a length of 769.33 feet and a breadth of 87.85, with a depth of 61.72. She was fore and aft rigged; she was fitted with six steam turbine engines of 65,000 indicated horse power, equal to a speed of 24 knots-that is, when all the boilers were working. She was registered at Liverpool, and her tonnage after deducting 17,784 tons for propelling power and crew space was 12,611. The ship was built under the special survey of the Admiralty and the Admiralty requirements. She had accommodation including the crew for over 3,000 persons." - Sir Edward Carson, a Member of Parliament and the King's Council, at the opening of the investigation into the loss of the *Lusitania*.

The *Lusitania* will forever be remembered as a result of the way in which it sank, but it's important to remember that the ship was, in many ways, a hybrid. For instance, the ship was built by a company named Cunard to be used as a passenger liner, much like the *Queen Mary* and the *Olympic* were. Cunard consisted of a group of investors who put a lot of money into the ship's construction in order to make it back, preferably with a profit, but the company also had a secret partner when they built the *Lusitania*. The ship's construction was supplemented by the government of Great Britain, with the understanding that should a war ever break out, the ship would be used by the government as an Armed Merchant Cruiser.

A picture with the *Olympic* in the front and the *Lusitania* in the background

According to Alexander Galbraith, a Superintending Engineer to the Cunard Line, the *Lusitania* was built to the highest specifications of the day: "The vessel was built throughout of steel and had a cellular double bottom of the usual type, with a floor at every frame, its depth at the center line being 60 inches, except in the way of turbine machinery, where it was 72 inches. This double bottom extended up the ship's side to a height of 8 feet above the keel. Above the double bottom the vessel was constructed on the usual transverse frame system, reinforced by web frames, which extended to the highest decks. At the forward end the framing and plating was strengthened with a view to preventing panting, and damage when meeting ice. Beams were fitted on every frame at all decks from the boat deck downwards. An external bilge keel about 300 feet long and 30 inches deep was fitted along the bilge amidships. The heavy plating was carried up to the shelter deck. Between the shelter deck and below the upper deck a depth of 14 feet 6 inches was double plated and hydraulic riveted. The stringer plate of the shelter deck was also doubled. All decks were steel plated throughout, The transverse strength of the ship was in part dependent on the 12 transverse watertight bulkheads which were specially strengthened and stiffened to enable them to stand the necessary pressure in the event of accident, and they were connected by double angles to decks, inner bottom and shell plating."

Likewise, the ship was powered by a state-of-the-art engine that was designed to allow the ship to move at speeds up to 28 knots (over 32 miles per hour), considered quite fast at the time. In fact, the *Lusitania*'s maximum speed, and what it took to make the ship move at top speed, would later be a major issue in the investigation surrounding the sinking. Galbraith added, "The main propelling machinery consisted of two high pressure ahead turbines, two low pressure ahead, and two astern turbines, driving four lines of main shafting. The two outer lines of shafting were each driven by a high pressure ahead turbine. The two inner lines of shafting were each driven by a low pressure ahead turbine. Forward of each low pressure ahead turbine and on the same line of shafting was an astern turbine, so that when going astern only the inner shafts were driving the ship. Steam was supplied by 23 double ended boilers and two single ended boilers, arranged for a working pressure of 195 lbs. per square inch."

The *Lusitania* before its launch

A picture of the *Lusitania's* First Class Drawing Room

A picture of the *Lusitania's* First Class Dining Room

Though the ship was built five years before the Titanic, the *Lusitania* had been the beneficiary of many improvements demanded by travelers following the *Titanic's* scandalous loss. As Sir Edward Carson pointed out, "She was fitted with 15 transverse bulkheads. The longest compartment was the forward boiler room, which was over 90 feet long, and all the watertight doors and the bulkheads could by special arrangements he closed simultaneously; and I think there is evidence that that was done on this occasion." The *Lusitania* also had what many felt would be enough to keep her afloat, a "double bottom, the depth between the outer and the inner being 5 feet at the center."

When the *Lusitania* made its maiden voyage, it surpassed everyone's expectations, and on its second voyage, it set the record for quickest transatlantic voyage by making finishing the trip in less than 5 days. Though the ship would not hold the record for long, its successes quickly made it a favorite on both sides of the Atlantic.

The Lusitania on its maiden voyage

The Lusitania sailing past Battery Park, New York City on its maiden trip

The Lusitania docking in *New York City* for the first time

A 1910 postcard featuring the *Lusitania* in New York City

Chapter 2: The Start of World War I

A picture of mail being delivered off the *Lusitania*

"She had aboard 4,200 cases of cartridges, but they were cartridges for small arms, packed in separate cases... they certainly do not come under the classification of ammunition. The United States authorities would not permit us to carry ammunition, classified as such by the military authorities, on a passenger liner. For years we have been sending small-arms cartridges abroad on the Lusitania." – Herman Winter, Assistant Manager of the Cunard Line, May 10, 1915

With the outbreak of World War I, the *Lusitania* was officially designated an Armed Merchant Cruiser, but at the same time, the ship continued to ply the waters as a civilian ocean liner, supposedly under the protection of the Cruiser Rules, a set of rules developed during the latter half of the 19th century to cover how civilian vessels would be treated during a time of war. The rules allowed for navies to capture an enemy's civilian ships, but if they did so, they had to provide safe passage for the non-military passengers on board. In the same vein, it forbade the targeting of civilian vessels by military ships.

The *Lusitania* continued to cross the Atlantic, a journey it made over 200 times by the middle of April 1915. Nonetheless, travel during wartime is always dangerous, and by then, everyone was nervous about what was going on in the Atlantic, primarily because of the newly designed German submarines that were patrolling the waters. The Germans were trying to prevent ships from reaching the coasts of the United Kingdom and let noncombatants know the zones in which their navies were operating.

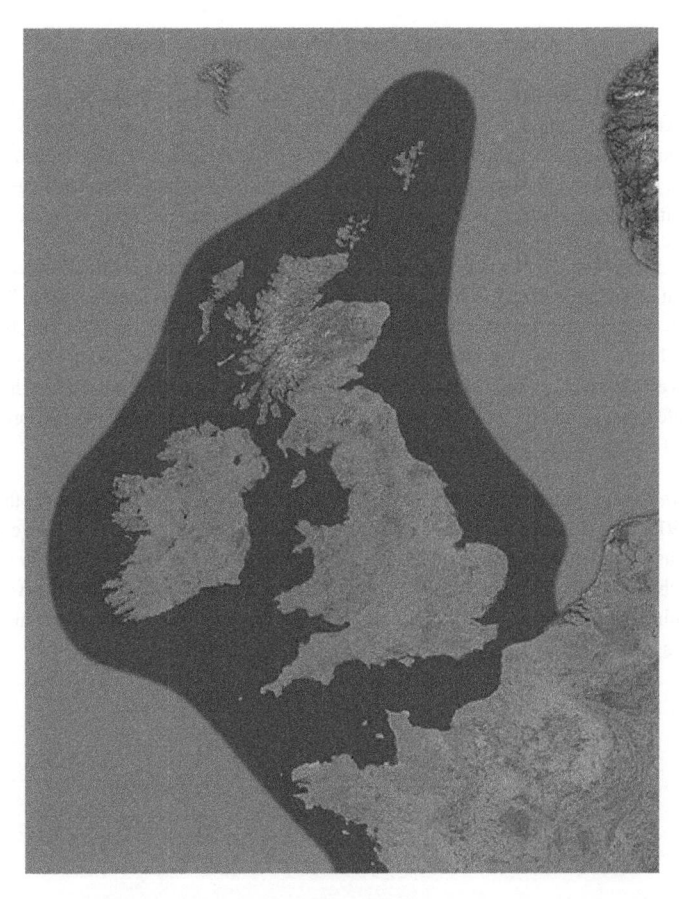

A map of the exclusion zone, a zone in which Germany claimed the right to attack or seize and search ships

At the urging of a number of concerned Americans of German heritage, the German Embassy in the United States went so far as to publish the following warning just days before the *Lusitania* left New York on what would be her final voyage:

> "NOTICE! TRAVELLERS intending to embark on the Atlantic voyage are reminded that a state of war exists between Germany and her allies and Great Britain and her allies; that the zone of war includes the waters adjacent to the British Isles; that, in accordance with formal notice given by the Imperial German Government, vessels flying the flag of Great Britain, or any of her allies, are liable

to destruction in those waters and that travelers sailing in the war zone on the ships of Great Britain or her allies do so at their own risk.
IMPERIAL GERMAN EMBASSY
Washington, D.C., April 22, 1915"

OCEAN STEAMSHIPS
CUNARD

EUROPE VIA LIVERPOOL
LUSITANIA

Fastest and Largest Steamer now in Atlantic Service Sails
SATURDAY, MAY 1, 10 A.M.
Transylvania, Fri., May 7, 5 P.M.
Orduña, - - Tues., May 18, 10 A.M.
Tuscania, - - Fri., May 21, 5 P.M.
LUSITANIA, Sat., May 29, 10 A.M.
Transylvania, Fri., June 4, 5 P.M.

Gibraltar—Genoa—Naples—Piraeus
S.S. Carpathia, Thur., May 13, Noon

NOTICE!

TRAVELLERS intending to embark on the Atlantic voyage are reminded that a state of war exists between Germany and her allies and Great Britain and her allies; that the zone of war includes the waters adjacent to the British Isles; that, in accordance with formal notice given by the Imperial German Government, vessels flying the flag of Great Britain, or of any of her allies, are liable to destruction in those waters and that travellers sailing in the war zone on ships of Great Britain or her allies do so at their own risk.

IMPERIAL GERMAN EMBASSY
WASHINGTON, D.C., APRIL 22, 1915.

The German Embassy's warning was printed alongside an advertisement for the *Lusitania*'s voyage

Woodrow Wilson's administration knew the Germans' U-boat policy and was already warning Germany not to target civilian ships, and on May 1, the very day that passengers were boarding the *Lusitania* on its trip back across the Atlantic, the president told Americans that "no warning that an unlawful and inhumane act will be committed" could justify actually conducting the attack. However, while many who boarded the *Lusitania* on May 1, 1915 had seen the German embassy's warning, most chose to disregard it, some for rather unusual reasons. For example, some believed that if the trip was truly dangerous, a warning would have been issued from a more reliable source than the Germans. Theodore Naish, traveling in Second Class with his wife, Belle, told her, "We will not worry. No reputable newspaper would accept an advertisement of that Cunard Line size and in it put another in direct opposition. It would be like advertising 'John Taylor Dry Goods Kansas City Missouri' and then inserting 'The Peck Dry Goods Company warns patrons of John Taylor Company as said goods are worthless or stolen.' If that were official, the notice would have been posted in glaring signs, and each American passenger would have had warning sent and delivered before boarding the vessel."

Others weren't about to let the danger or warnings scare them off. Phoebe Amory later admitted, "[I]t is only natural, and not to be attributed to a desire to boast, that I should have made the voyage warning or no warning."

Of course, many passengers understandably found the German warning worrisome, including Reverend Clark, who later recalled the trepidation he experienced even as he was booking his passage on the ship: "I only asked the man who gave me my ticket whether there was any extraordinary danger in travelling by the *Lusitania* and he told me, no, there was none as far as he knew, and that the Cunard Company were not likely to risk a ship of such enormous value if there was any extra danger. [Staff Captain James Clarke Anderson] told me almost at the beginning of the voyage that six of the boilers had been cut off and that the result of that was that 1000 tons of coal would be saved on the voyage and I asked him a question or two…I asked him if that was altogether giving us the best chance, and his answer was that as the Germans had not succeeded in torpedoing any vessel that was going more than 12 knots an hour, and as the *Lusitania* with the boilers which were in commission could comfortably go 21 or 22 knots, it was considered that there was an ample margin of safety."

The changes Reverend Clark was referencing were made in response to the outbreak of the war and the shortages in both fuel and manpower that the fighting had brought. Not only were many young men who might otherwise have fired engines on civilian crafts joining the Navy, the coal used in luxury liners was also needed for naval ships. Alfred Allen Booth, Chairman of the Cunard Line, later explained, "That change was made, not at the outbreak of the war, but in November, I think. After the rush of homeward - bound American traffic was over, and that came to an end towards the end of October, it became a question as to whether we could continue running the two large steamers the *Lusitania* and the 'Mauretania' at all or not. We went into the matter very carefully and we came to the conclusion that it would be possible to continue running one of them at a reduced speed, that is to say, that the traffic would be sufficient, but only sufficient to justify running one steamer a month if we reduced the expense. To run it to pay expenses. We did not hope to make any profit, and as a matter of fact we did not make any profit. We decided to run the *Lusitania*, not the 'Mauretania,' at ¾ - boiler power, and that meant a reduction of speed from an average of about 24 knots to an average of about 21 knots. It would result in a considerable reduction in the total consumption of coal, and also a reduction in the number of men required for the crew, both of which were important."

The *Mauretania* and *Lusitania*

While the changes did result in savings, passengers such as Clark were worried that they might also make the *Lusitania* a sitting duck for the German submarines. Booth later had to answer these allegations, as well as explain the measures he and the other leaders of the Cunard Line took to respond to the published German threat. He explained, "I do not think I heard anything about the special threats made in New York until the Sunday morning after she had sailed. I have been trying to remember whether I heard on the Saturday. I cannot remember whether I did, but I understand the threats were published in New York on the Saturday morning. Therefore, I do not think I could have heard until the Saturday evening at the earliest. I certainly remember knowing it on the Sunday but not on the Saturday. I should not generally put a subject of that kind down for specific discussion at a Board Meeting or a Committee Meeting of Directors. I am in constant touch with them every day and with my Managers, and I have no recollection now of any specific discussion on that point, I am quite sure if there had been we should have felt that we could not make any difference in our action. It was a question of either running the *Lusitania* at 21 knots or not running her at all; and I know my own view would have been strongly against withdrawing the ship entirely on the submarine threat, and I think that I must in conversation with my Directors have learned that that was also their view. Certainly, it was taken for granted as far as I am concerned."

In Booth's mind, the most important thing was that the captains of the individual ships in the line be made aware of what was going on. He felt that they would then be the best judges about how to proceed based on their years of experience and training: "We discussed the submarine danger with the individual captains - either I or my immediate assistant in every case, but the discussion had necessarily to be of the nature of making sure that they realized what the general dangers were. We could not venture to give specific instructions when in an emergency they would be in possession of facts which could not be in our possession, and we felt it would be very dangerous to attempt to give specific instructions when the circumstances might make those instructions absolutely dangerous to follow. ... We discussed the general form the danger would take and the general methods whereby it could best be avoided. One of the particular points of course was the question of closing the watertight doors when in the danger zone, swinging out the boats, seeing that all the ports were closed, seeing that everything was ready in the boats; and another point was the danger of stopping in the danger zone to pick up a pilot or stopping at the Liverpool Bar to wait for the tide to rise."

Tragically, the dangers would soon be realized.

Chapter 3: Bound for Liverpool

A 1908 photo of the *Lusitania* headed for Liverpool

"*The steamship Lusitania which was both a passenger ship and an emigrant ship … belonging to the Cunard Line, was, at the end of April, at New York, and was about to sail for England on the first of May. She left New York about noon on the 1st of May with a crew, …a large number of passengers, and a general cargo, bound for Liverpool…On the morning of the 6th May…all the Class A lifeboats, amounting to 22, were swung outwards under the superintendence of the proper officer and were left swinging and ready for lowering.*" - Sir Edward Carson

Early in the morning of May 1, 1915, more than 600 blurry-eyed seamen made their way onto the *Lusitania* to prepare the ship for departure. All but 25 of them were men, and they were mostly young adults who had signed up for a life at sea in the hopes of seeing the world and having a few adventures. In fact, many of them had been up drinking late into the night and were now trying to sober up enough to do their jobs. They joined those who had stood watch through the night to make up the ship's full complement of 702. About 300 reported to the ship's engine rooms to prepare for launch later that day, while another 300 busied themselves checking staterooms and dining saloons to make sure all was in readiness for the passenger's comfort. The rest scattered throughout the ship to do their assigned tasks.

A few hours after the last crewman was aboard, the passengers started to board. As was the practice at the time, the Third Class (steerage) passengers made their way to their cabins through their own entrance, separate from the entrance set aside for the First and Second Class passengers. About 600 men, women and children headed to steerage, and the other 660 passengers boarding the ship were divided pretty evenly between First Class and steerage. The ship itself was well-designed and cared for, with much thought having been given to the passengers' comfort. Theodore Diamandis, a steerage passenger from Greece, later mentioned, "There is not any promenade deck in the third class on the port side. It is an entrance to the second class. … That deck is a long deck for the third class passengers to promenade and the other is for the second class passengers. That is the long deck - the promenade deck."

Following the loss of the *Titanic* three years earlier, there had been an increase in both the number of lifeboat drills required for an ocean liner and in the passengers' interest in them. Reverend Clark observed a drill not long after he boarded the ship: "At 11 o'clock there was a bell rung and there was a boat which was kept swung out all the time during the voyage as far as I know, and a number of men came and got into the boat, put on lifebelts for a few seconds and took them off again, the boat not being moved all this time; then they jumped out of the boat and ran back." While strides had definitely been made since the sinking of the *Titanic*, which took 3 hours to sink after striking an iceberg, the additional lifeboat drills would prove to be insufficient preparation for a torpedoed ship that sank in less than 20 minutes.

A picture of passengers and collapsible lifeboats on the *Lusitania*

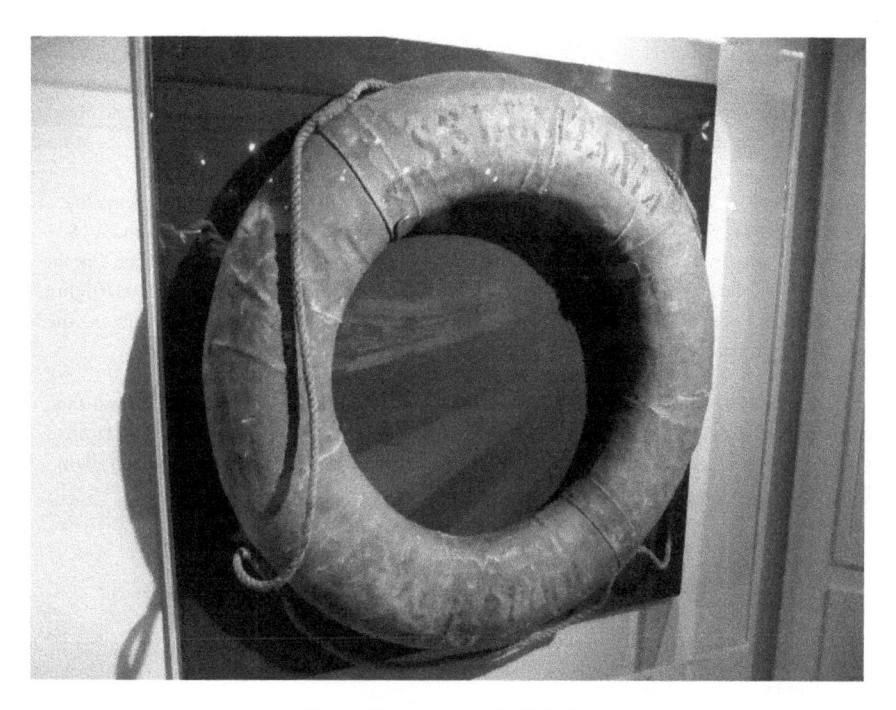

One of the *Lusitania*'s lifebelts

For the most part, the voyage was uneventful, but as the *Lusitania* approached the English coast, the ship's captain and crew became more cautious. The shore near Liverpool was considered particularly dangerous because so many submarines had been spotted in the area. In describing the recommendations Cunard had given her captains, Booth said, "It was one of the points that we felt it necessary to make the Captain of the *Lusitania* understand the importance of. The *Lusitania* can only cross the Liverpool Bar at certain states of the tide, and we therefore warned the captain, or whoever might be captain, that we did not think it would be safe for him to arrive off the bar at such a time that he would have to wait there, because that area had been infested with submarines, and we thought therefore it would be wiser for him to arrange his arrival in such a way, leaving him an absolutely free hand as to how he would do it, that he could come straight up without stopping at all. The one definite instruction we did give him with regard to that was to authorize him to come up without a pilot."

On the morning of May 7, passengers who paid attention to such things would have noticed that the lifeboats had been uncovered and swung out to the sides of the ship. If any took the time to ask a crewman why this had been done, they might not have liked the answer. Sir Edward Carson explained, "That was in consequence of the ship then approaching what may be called the war zone or the danger zone. About 10 minutes past 2 p.m. on the 7th May the vessel was off the Irish Coast. She had passed early in the morning the Fastnet Rock at the extreme corner where you turn round to come up the Irish Channel, and had arrived at 2.10 near the Old Head of Kinsale. …The ship was about 8 to 10 miles off the Old Head of Kinsale. One of the questions which will arise on the evidence is as to whether that was, at the time and under the circumstances which your Lordship will hear, a proper place for the captain to be navigating. The weather was fine and clear and the sea was smooth and the vessel was making about 18 knots." The passengers could not have known it, but all the watertight bulkheads located in the lower parts of the ship had also been closed and sealed. Ironically, the fact that the watertight compartments were closed ahead of time meant some crewmen would be trapped in them when the ship was torpedoed and thus had no chance to escape the sinking ship.

One of the things that came out during the investigation of the loss of the *Lusitania* was that, considering the dangerous water in which he found himself, Captain William Thomas Turner was charting a rather relaxed course, as indicated by the conversation between him and Clem Edwards, a representative of the seamen's union:

"Edwards: At the time you were struck were you steering a perfectly straight course?
Turner: As straight as you can steer.

Edwards: To get that maximum speed how many of the boilers had to be fired?
Turner: Twenty-five.

Edwards: At the time you were struck how many of the boilers were in fact fired?
Turner: Nineteen.

Edwards: Was it a matter within your discretion, or was it in consequence of orders from your owners that you bad only nineteen of your boilers fired?
Turner: Orders of the owners.

Edwards: So that at that time if you had thought it the right thing to keep full speed ahead you could not have attained anywhere the maximum speed of 24 to 25 knots?
Turner: No; 21.

Captain Turner

Donald MacMaster, representing Canadian interests, also had some questions about this issue.

"MacMaster: On the morning of the 7th May were you aware that you were in a danger zone?
Turner: I was.

MacMaster: And that you might possibly be subject to a torpedo attack?
Turner: Yes.

MacMaster: Did you give any special instructions or take any special precautions with a view to observing whether submarines where in the neighborhood on the morning of the 7th May?
Turner: I did. I gave orders to the engineers in case I rang full speed ahead to give her extra speed.

MacMaster: Did you give orders to look out for submarines?
Turner: The look-outs were already doubled."

These precautions would prove completely insufficient on May 7, 1915.

Chapter 4: "A Million-Ton Hammer"

"Without any warning a German submarine fired a torpedo at the *Lusitania* and she was struck between the third and fourth funnels. There is evidence that there was a second and perhaps a third torpedo fired, and the ship sank within 20 minutes…there was no possibility under the circumstances of making any immediate preparation to save the lives of the passengers on board…the course adopted by the German Government was not only contrary to International law and the usages of war, but was contrary to the dictates of civilization and humanity; and to have sunk the passengers under those circumstances and under the conditions that I have stated meant in the eye, not only of our law but of every other law that I know of in civilized countries, a deliberate attempt to murder the passengers on board that ship." - Sir Edward Carson

"It sounded like a million-ton hammer hitting a steam boiler a hundred feet high." – A passenger on the *Lusitania*

Around 11:00 a.m. on May 7, the British Admiralty issued a warning for ships near the coast: "U-boats active in southern part of Irish Channel. Last heard of twenty miles south of Coningbeg Light Vessel." This warning was due in part to the fact that a German submarine, U-20, had fired torpedoes at several ships in the area the day before, sinking two of them. Around 1:00 p.m., ships in the area received another warning: "Submarine five miles south of Cape Clear proceeding west when sighted at 10:00 am." Unfortunately, that warning was inaccurate, and it also had the effect of making the *Lusitania*'s captain think it had already passed a German submarine.

A picture of German submarines at Kiel, with U-20 second from left

By the morning of May 7, the *Lusitania* had already started taking noticeable precautions, including using depth soundings to try detecting enemy U-boats. It had slowed down due to heavy fog in the morning, but as the fog cleared closer to noon, the *Lusitania* picked its speed back up to 18 knots (20 miles per hour).

As fate would have it, the *Lusitania* would be sighted by the same German submarine, U-20, that sank a couple of ships the day before, and one of the reasons the two crossed paths is because the German submarine was low on fuel and torpedoes and was thus heading for home. Still, with 3 torpedoes left, U-20's commander, Walther Schwieger, could target at least one more ship. His first attempted target, the cruiser *Juno*, passed the U-boat around noon but was traveling fast and zigzagging to make it harder for a submarine to target the ship. As a result, the U-20 never got a shot off at the cruiser.

Schwieger

Shortly before 1:30 p.m., the U-20 sighted a large steamer and submerged in order to advance toward it. The submarine began to tail its target, but by moving at 18 knots, the *Lusitania* could move faster than the U-boat, and no merchant ship or ocean liner moving faster than 15 knots had ever been sunk by a submarine. While it was not moving near its top speed, the *Lusitania* could still outrun the submarine, and given its course, Schwieger thought for a time that his U-20 would never get close enough to actually fire a torpedo at the *Lusitania*.

Of course, the *Lusitania*'s advantage in speed could only help if Captain Turner and the crew knew of the location of the submarine, but nobody on board even knew one was present. As a result, less than an hour after U-20 spotted the ship, a change in the *Lusitania*'s course brought it into range for a torpedo attack. Around 2:10 p.m., with his submarine less than half a mile away from the steamer, Schwieger ordered a torpedo to be fired at the target. He wrote in his submarine's log, "Torpedo hits starboard side right behind the bridge. An unusually heavy detonation takes place with a very strong explosive cloud. The explosion of the torpedo must have been followed by a second one [boiler or coal or powder?]... The ship stops immediately and heels over to starboard very quickly, immersing simultaneously at the bow... the name Lusitania becomes visible in golden letters." Raimund Weisbach, U-20's torpedo officer, also indicated his surprise at the extent of the explosion and the fact that the *Lusitania*'s forecastle (the foremost section of the upper deck forward of the mast) was already below water in less than 10 minutes.

A depiction of where the torpedo hit the ship and the damage caused by the explosion

This German depiction of the explosion incorrectly has the torpedo hitting the port side instead of the starboard side

A more accurate depiction of the *Lusitania* listing to its starboard side as it sank

The torpedo that struck the *Lusitania* was traveling at a depth of only 3 meters, making it possible to notice on board the steamer. Joseph Casey, a fireman on the ship, was one of the extra watchmen Turner ordered to keep a look out for submarines, and while he never saw U-20 itself, he recognized the torpedo. Turner later asserted, "We were given instructions how to recognize a torpedo when it was coming through the water. ... [I was] on the starboard side between the after-end of the engineers' quarters and the commencement of the second class cabins. There was another shipmate of mine and me looking at a passenger fixing a trunk up, and this shipmate says to me, 'Joe, what's that?' I immediately looked to the forward end on the starboard side and I saw two white streaks approaching the ship; one seemed to be travelling quicker than the other. At the beginning I thought there was only one, but as they approached the ship they opened outwards and the after one seemed to strike the ship either forward or near the center of No.2 funnel, and a white flash came and an explosion. There seemed to be two explosions but they were like together. ... [Later] when we were getting ready to go down the rope to go over the side aft, there was this streak of a third torpedo coming from a diagonal direction. On the starboard side. It was fired from the forward end on the starboard side, not the same as the others in a straight line, but in a diagonal line."

A British depiction shows a second torpedo hitting the *Lusitania* near the hole left by the first

A diagram showing where the (alleged) two torpedoes hit the *Lusitania*

As Casey's testimony suggests, there would be a subsequent debate over how many torpedoes had been fired. Casey insisted that there were at least 3 torpedoes fired by the U-boat, with the first two hitting and the third missing, but this is contradicted by Schwieger's account. In fact, as the *Lusitania* was in the process of sinking, Schwieger wrote down, "It looks as if the ship will stay afloat only for a very short time. [I gave order to] dive to 25 metres and leave the area seawards. I couldn't have fired another torpedo into this mass of humans desperately trying to save themselves."

Regardless of the number of torpedoes fired, most of the passengers had no idea what was going on until they felt the sudden lurch in the ship and heard the explosion, and even then, most did not know what had actually happened until they were on the lifeboats and the situation was explained to them. Reverend Clark described how the impact had thrown him to the ground: "I had come up from lunch in the lift and had gone up to the smoking room, and then, walking through the smoke room, got on to what is called the verandah. Outside the smoking room in the open air, and looking straight aft, and I was talking to an American there when the explosion took place. I did not see the torpedo, but I saw the impact, and the immediate result of the impact saw that it shook the vessel, as far as I could make out, from stem to stern, and I saw a quantity of water at once pouring down. I suppose it had been thrown up by the force of the explosion, and was coming back again, and almost immediately it seemed to me that the list to starboard started. There was a violent explosion along with the impact. I should find it very difficult to describe, because it was only momentary. I do not think I can say that I saw any smoke or anything of that sort. I felt the impact. I thought at first that it was a mine that we had struck, as I did not see the torpedo."

John Freeman, a Second Class passenger, was relaxing on deck with his wife but did not see the cause of the explosion. He discussed the initial shock and confusion: "We were sitting on the promenade deck looking at the coast of Ireland and there was this explosion. It seemed to me to be in front near the first funnel and I said to my wife, 'that is a mine' - thinking we were running on to a mine, I did not think that we should be torpedoed without any warning. We stood looking, and immediately there was a second explosion, and that was followed by hot water and steam, and it seemed to me that there were cinders as well. The second explosion took place near to the first one, and that caused a little confusion and alarm, and we stepped into the lounge to get out of the way of the steam and hot water. The second lunch was on, and the passengers came rushing up from the dining saloon, and they had only just started lowering the boats. … As soon as we crossed the gangway the people went up towards the port side almost every one of them, and I said to my wife 'We will go the other way,' and we lost our foothold immediately going down from the gangway of the vessel, and we slid down the side of the vessel. I saw about half-way down the first class promenade deck some sailors preparing to lower the boat. I thought they seemed to know their business and I noticed, that they were regular seamen, at least so it seemed to me from their jerseys. We got our feet again but the list was so great that we fell down again although we were only walking on the promenade deck, but I held on to the railing and supported my wife and got her into the boat."

While most passengers only knew that something dramatic had happened, Theodore Diamandis had the dubious honor of being one of the few passengers to see U-20. His testimony would prove crucial in the investigation surrounding the attack: "Myself and two friends of mine, two Greeks, went down and we could not get second class cabins, and we were obliged to take third class cabins. At the time she was struck we had finished lunch about half-past one, and I sat about 20 or 25 minutes talking to my friends, and then I thought of going round to have a shave in the second class. On my arrival at the barber's shop, about 30 or 40 yards on the other side, she was struck immediately. After she was struck I ran aft towards the First Class, when I went up on the top deck, and when the *Lusitania* was turning towards the land, then I saw the periscope of the submarine just disappearing. I should say about 300 yards [away]. … Well, when I was going round to the port side and when I went upstairs on to the port deck, the *Lusitania* had then practically turned a semicircle toward the shore and from the port side you could then see the periscope from there. … I have no experience of periscopes, but I have seen them. I know what the conning tower is. It is the larger part of the submarine. … If it was the conning tower that the people went down into the submarine, that is what I call the conning tower."

For his part, Captain Turner had years of experience at sea, including some time spent training in naval warfare. Therefore, he was able to provide more details of the incident, including what he did in response to the first explosion: "The officer called out 'There is a torpedo coming, sir,' and I went across to the starboard side and saw the wake, and there was immediately an explosion and the ship took a heavy list. [On] the starboard side. A big volume of smoke and steam came up between the third and fourth funnels, counting from forward-I saw that myself. I saw a streak like the wake of a torpedo."

Although the *Lusitania* ended up sinking much faster than anyone expected, including the German submarine crew, there was an initial hope that it might stay above water for awhile. Albert Arthur Bestwick, a Junior Third Officer on the *Lusitania*, explained, "I heard an explosion. I was in the officers' smoke room at the time, and I went out on the bridge and I saw the track of a torpedo. It seemed to be fired in a line with the bridge, and it seemed to strike the ship between the second and third funnels, as far as I could see. Then I heard the order given 'hard-a-starboard' and I heard Captain Turner saying 'lower the boats down level to the rail,' and I went to my section of boats. My boat station was No. 10 on the port side. That was my individual boat; my section was from 2 to 10. I started to get No. 10 lowered down to the rail, but it landed on the deck. Captain Anderson was there beside me and he said: 'Go to the bridge and tell them they are to trim her with the port tanks.' I made my way to the bridge and sung out that order to Mr. Heppert, the second officer. He repeated it and I came back again and No. 10 boat was on the deck. We tried to push it out, but we could not do it. [The ship] had a big list to starboard on her. ... Captain Anderson was there beside me and I took most of my orders from him. I thought when we trimmed her with the port tanks she might right herself a little bit. She went on listing for about 10 minutes I should say. Then she seemed to rectify the list a little bit. ... When she rectified herself a little bit it gave us encouragement and we thought she might come up altogether or it might give us a better chance."

Since the *Lusitania* was only 15 miles from shore at that moment, Turner's first thought was that if he pushed the ship's engines, he could speed to land before the vessel sank. This was often possible with larger ships because a small hole would not allow enough water in to sink them immediately. However, he quickly realized that was not an option: "I headed her for the land to see if I could make the land. [I] ordered the boats to be lowered down to the rails, to get the women and children in first. [I] put her head on to the land, and then I saw she had a lot of way on her and was not sinking, so I put her full speed astern, to take the way off her. ... [I realized] that the engines were out of commission."

Meanwhile, First Officer Arthur Jones was dealing with his own crisis. He was one of only a few stewards present in a large room of passengers who were quickly flying into a panic. He later related his experience: "Well, when we were struck there were about 100 people lunching in the saloon, and the moment she was struck of course we all got up and they preceded me out through both doors. I was about the last man to come out of the saloon. It was as I was passing through the door that I issued this order, 'Close the ports if any are open.' ... I simply told the people to be calm on the way up, and to be as collected as they possibly could."

Closing the porthole windows proved to be important, because as the ship immediately began to list to the side, it placed many of the windows on the starboard side under water. Had the windows not been closed and sealed, the water would have rushed in that much more quickly and sink the ship even faster. Carson explained, "The torpedo which struck the ship, ...struck her on the starboard side. That caused an immediate list on the ship, which, if it did momentarily right itself, afterwards increased, and was of such a nature...that it made the boats on the port side practically impossible to launch. Some of them I think were filled with passengers, but, as your Lordship will readily imagine, in the few moments that elapsed these boats with the list over fell in-board and some of them fell over upon some of the passengers on the deck."

Chapter 5: Abandoning Ship

"The Lusitania was a passenger steamer and an emigrant ship as defined by Sections 267 and 268 of the Merchant Shipping Act, and as a passenger ship she had to be surveyed annually for the passengers' certificate, and as an emigrant ship, every voyage before clearance outwards. ... She also had to comply with the rules as to life-saving appliances, which had to be surveyed under the 431st section of the Act. There were also special instructions which are not statutory which were given by the Company as regards boat drills...The Lusitania held a passenger certificate enabling her to carry 400 passengers of each class, that would be 1,200 altogether, and a crew of 750 hands. She was certified to have, and had as a matter of fact, on board, 34 boats, capable of accommodating 1,950 persons. She had 32 lifebuoys and 2,325 life-jackets. ... The ship...seems in every way to have fulfilled the requirements of the law and the regulations that were laid down." - Sir Edward Carson

Unable to get his passengers to shore, Captain Turner next attempted to offload them into lifeboats, knowing that the survivors would soon be picked up if they could just stay afloat. However, he soon found there were problems with this plan as well: "I told them to hold on lowering the boats till the way was off the ship a bit, which was done. I told the staff captain to lower the boats when he thought the way was sufficiently off to allow them to be lowered. They could not very well lower them on the port side because of the heavy list [of] I should say about 15 degrees. They caught on the rail and capsized some of the people out. Some were let go on the run, and some of them fell inboard on the deck and hurt some of the passengers. I said 'All women and children into the boats first,' and I told them to lower them down to the rails."

Unlike the infamous *Titanic*, the *Lusitania* had plenty of lifeboats, and the maritime rules passed following the loss of the former guaranteed that there would be more than enough lifeboats to hold both the passengers and the crew. However, getting the passengers into them proved to be more difficult than anyone had anticipated. Robert Cairns, a passenger from First Class, later complained, "As a matter of fact had it not been for the passengers the [lifeboat] would never have been in the water at all; it was entirely owing to the passengers. I am pretty strong and I got right into the center, and I went back five or six paces, and I said to the others, 'The moment I rush the boat to the center, push like wild' and we were just able to get the boat over, and then I got all the women and children into the boat. I said 'women and children must go into the boat first and men afterwards.' ... She commenced to leak immediately, and there were five or six gentlemen with their hats doing their very utmost to bale her out, and just in a few moments she was right full of water level to the sea. ... When I saw the boat was level with the sea, and everyone, of course, was expecting the boat to go down every minute; I am a very good swimmer, and I jumped out immediately, and I was followed by another passenger. I had been swimming for about a minute and a half, and I had turned round to look at the boat, and the boat had gone down, capsized, with the keel upwards. All had gone down with it with the exception of two or three who were hanging on to the keel."

Though several passengers would subsequently complain that the officers and seamen alike were poorly trained and inefficient, it's only fair to note that most of the crewmen were trying to do their best under almost impossible circumstances; after all, they had never trained in launching lifeboats off of a ship that was nearly on its side in the water. Moreover, Diamandis recalled seeing lifeboats being launched in an orderly fashion: "I crossed the boat deck to the starboard side. ... There were three boats in that pat just swung in the davits and they were lowering them down and there was an officer there attending to it…giving instructions to the crew to help the people. ... I did not see any stewards, but on the deck where I was there was an officer giving instructions, and there were two or three people helping the women and children into the boats."

Naturally, no matter how trained the crew was, the attack was so sudden and violent that there was more panic than order throughout the ship. One passenger, James Baker, described some of the bedlam that many passengers experienced: "I was in my cabin, and when I got up they were lowering - I could not tell you the number-the boats opposite the leading room on the port side. I remained on the port side the whole time. I think-I am sure it was opposite the reading room, and I saw that boat run away because the man at the bows could not hold the falls. At the stern the rope fouled and left the boat bows in the water, and at an angle of about 45 degrees. There was a young officer in the water when I looked over. I did not see the start of lowering the boat, but when I looked over to see what had happened, there was a young officer trying to climb into the bows. The stern post had been wrenched away from the sides, so that when the boat did get into the water she could not possibly keep afloat. I know there was a bit of a list. When I got on to the deck there was a greater list than later on. The ship appeared to me to gradually right herself, because when I got to the second boat we were able to shove the boat out and had got her clear when we got orders to clear the boats, all women to come out."

Baker then went on to describe how the atmosphere of the ship's deck quickly broke out in chaos, due largely to the fact that the *Lusitania* was going down so fast. Discussing his efforts to help load a lifeboat on the port side of the ship, he continued, "We had filled her with women and children and we were trying to shove her out, the list having brought the boat in. We stood on the collapsible boat and tried to shove her out, and while we were attempting to do it the list was so great that the number of men there at the time could not do it. We called for more men; we had not much purchase as we were standing on top of the collapsible boat, but finally we got steady and with one shove got her clear and lowered her a foot or so, when the order came 'Stop lowering the boat. Clear the boat,' and we got everyone out."

Having realized that there was little more he could do where he was, Baker decided to go to another part of the ship and offer his services there: "I came then to very nearly the smoke room and they were at work launching a boat there; but as there seemed to be plenty of men, I started on the collapsible boat and did not attempt to help with the third boat. I heard it run away and collapse and smash up like a matchbox. May I say with regard to the second boat, while that was being lowered I came to the conclusion that there were not enough men in the boat to help shove her off the side as she ran down. I made it five men, but I will not swear to it. When I saw the boats going down and they could not hold them, I realized that it was a question of moments. I looked round to see what was being done with the collapsible boats, and I could not see one being got ready nor the canvas tops taken off, so with a penknife I cut one clear and was working on a second when I saw the water coming."

Others, despairing of finding a place on a lifeboat, began to prepare to go in the water, which obviously required donning a lifebelt. Somewhat surprisingly, many of the passengers never even tried to put theirs on, hoping instead to find a place on a lifeboat, but Reverend Clark decided it would be wise to take the time to find a life preserver to put on. He recalled, "I waited for a minute, and then I went down to my cabin on the D deck, [but there] was no lifebelt properly so-called, it was a sort of jacket. I believe it was called Boddy's Patent Jacket. … [Then] went first to the port side. My cabin was on the starboard side but I groped my way back with very great difficulty…and I got first on to the port side for a moment, and I saw a man from a great height throw himself into the water and come down what seemed to me to be a fearful smash, and I saw another boat which was half lowered and the falls then seemed to get jammed. …A great number of people in that boat were spilled into the water, and I walked back then to the starboard side. … Eventually I got into a boat on the starboard side. … Well, when we got into the boat two of the funnels were hanging over that side and threatening to smash the boats up. I attempted to get into a boat before, but there was a woman with a child in the boat, and she was afraid of me, perhaps, jumping near her, and she screamed to me not to jump, and so I went on to what I imagined to be the last boat there. … We were so tightly packed that it was impossible to move the oars at first, and I thought the funnels would come down."

Not everyone who went back to his room to grab a life preserver was so fortunate. John Freeman, a Second Class Passenger, discovered something very eerie when he went below decks: "When I went to deck 'E' it was in darkness owing to the electric light being out, apart from a little light which came in from the port-holes on the port side of the vessel. The starboard side was entirely in darkness. I did not realize at the time that the vessel was under water, but these port-holes normally are just above the water-line."

Unlike the rumors that plagued the *Titanic*, there were no accusations among those housed in steerage that they were prevented from getting off the ship. Indeed, Joseph Frankum described how he and his family made their escape: "We were all having a cup of tea for'ard, just after getting our baggage ready for shore... something went bang. I knew what it was immediately. The vessel at once heeled over to starboard, and my little boy turned and said, 'What's that, Daddy?' I didn't answer him... As soon as the explosion occurred, I gripped my two boys while my wife took charge of the little girl... I wouldn't wait to get lifebelts, as I was afraid we should get trapped below."

Instead, they quickly made their way to the upper deck. Frankum continued, "In the hurry, I dropped my little boy who fell about six feet, but I picked him up again and we made our way towards one of the boats... I pushed the wife and kiddies into a boat and said, 'You stay there while I try and get a lifebelt... I shall be alright.' Then I made for the second cabin saloon and got a couple of the lifebelts. Remembering that my people were already in the boat, I said, 'Here, old man, take this.' [to a man who did not have a lifebelt]. When I got back to the deck, I found the missus and the children had got out of the boat. The steamer had got a heavy list, but just then she steadied a bit and I thought she might right herself... She started to heel over again. I said to my wife 'Oh my God, it's all over. Get back into the lifeboat again.'"

By then, it was too late, and the water was coming up over the deck. Frankum explained his futile attempt to hold onto his family: "I hoped that as she sank the lifeboat might rise in her chocks, but whether it did or not I don't know, for the next instant I was wrenched from my hold and hurled into the water... I stuck to my wife and children as long as I could, but as we sank, we were separated... I was sucked down very deep but came to the surface again. I could find no traces of my wife nor any of the children." At that point, he managed to get himself into another lifeboat: "A young gentleman who was on the boat tried to comfort me for the loss of my family, and while he was so engaged a man's body floated alongside us. The young gentleman picked up an oar and lifted the head of the dead man. 'Good God,' he cried, 'It's my own father.' And then I had to comfort him."

In the end, Frankum would learn that only one of his three children, his son Francis, had survived.

Chapter 6: Total Loss

"The Track of Lusitania," a 1915 illustration depicting bodies and survivors in the wake of the sinking

"The total crew was 702, made up of deck department 77, engineering department 314, stewards 306, the orchestra 5; that made 702. Of these, there were 677 males and 25 females. 397 males and 16 females were lost; therefore, the total loss of the crew was 413; 280 males and 9 females were saved. Those figures make up the 702. The total passengers were 1,257, made up of saloon passengers 290, second -cabin passengers 600, third- cabin passengers 367, making a total of 1,257. Of these there were 688 adult males, 440 adult females, 51 male children, and 39 female children, and 39 infants. The number of passengers lost was 785, and the number saved 472. Of the 129 children, 94 were lost and 35 saved." - Sir Edward Carson

Given the rapid chain of events, most of the passengers on board the *Lusitania* never even had a chance to make it to a lifeboat or even get back to their rooms and don lifebelts. According to First Officer Jones, "After I had lowered No. 15 in the water I then went down the fall myself a few seconds afterwards, and the boat deck was level with the water. A matter of 15 seconds; it was not half a minute. Well, she started with her head to starboard and then she went down by the head herself, and, I take it, as far as I can judge, she upended herself until her nose touched the bottom and then she sank down herself. I should say she had an angle of about 30 degrees from the perpendicular."

To a world that had barely recovered from the shocking loss of the Titanic a few years earlier, the loss of the *Lusitania* came as a terrible blow. While the death tolls in each disaster were nearly equal, there were aspects of the *Lusitania's* sinking that made it so much more offensive to the human psyche. For one thing, the ship went down very fast, going from sailing on the sea to sitting at the bottom 300 feet below in less than 20 minutes. This meant that those who did survive had little time to even come to terms with what was happening. Furthermore, there was the fact that the *Lusitania* was deliberately sunk, not the result of a tragic but accidental disaster.

Even for those who made it to lifeboats, there was still plenty of danger, and many who thought they had reached the safety of the small crafts were instead suddenly plunged to their deaths. David Alfred Thomas, one of the passengers from First Class, later complained, "I would say that there was no kind of organization, but there was certainly panic five or ten minutes after the boat was struck, and I do not think the order of the captain, 'women and children first,' was obeyed by a very large number of the crew. They looked after themselves first - they took care to save themselves first - in fact I met two or three of them afterwards, and they were boasting about it at Queenstown. I know at the time the first boat sank - it is not direct evidence - there were very few women and children in the boat that I got into. The first boat on the port side was let down so badly that the whole of the passengers and crew that were in it fell into the water - there were very few women in that. … I was going to say that of course the Court can ascertain for themselves probably the figures of those saved, the different classes, women and children, and the first, second, and third class passengers and crew. With regard to the first boat, I was told by a number of people in the first boat that it was let down more rapidly than the others, that was on the port side, and the whole of those in the boat were plunged into the water, and my daughter, who was close by me, told me that there were very few in that boat and that there were not more than half a dozen children in that boat."

Another factor that made the sinking of the *Lusitania* shocking to the entire world was the many nationalities represented among the victims. While most of the passengers on board were from Great Britain, Canada or the United States, there were people lost from a total of 20 different countries, covering every populated continent in the world. Many of the losses were also infamous because of the popularity or notoriety of so many of those killed. For instance, the popular opera singer Millie Baker, then only 27 years old, lost her life. The American playwright and actor Charles Klein was drowned, along with producer Charles Frohman and novelist Justus Forman. The three were on their way back to England from America, where they had been looking for a backer for a new play based on Forman's novel, *The Hyphen*. Forman's obituary summed up his life and work: "When the *Lusitania* sank, finis was written to his last story, and now his career is as a tale that is told. No account of his final great adventure has come back from the scene of his tragic close. Those to whom his coming was a pleasure and who will never again welcome him, can only surmise that he met his end calmly and without dismay or fear, as an American gentleman should, and that came to his comfort and support that dominating vital sense which characterized his life and will ever be associated with his memory in the mind of his friends. He must have died as one who goes forth expectantly and wholly unafraid in quest of lands unknown, but filled with possibilities of happy venturing."

Forman

There were hundreds of heart-wrenching stories, such as that of the Aitken family: James, 57, Jarvie, 32, and James Jarvie, 2. They were traveling back to England after burying Jarvie's young wife, Grace, in Canada, and all three generations went down together. Then there were the Allen's, consisting of mother Marguerite and her two daughters, Anna and Gwen. When the ship went down, the girls fell into the ocean, and Marguerite then jumped in with them, crying out that they should all die together. Instead, she survived and lived on with the memory of her two children dying before her eyes. Mr. and Mrs. Walter Bailey drowned along with their daughter, Ivy, leaving behind their son, 14 year old Albert Victor.

One of the strangest losses was that of Lindon Bates, a well-known author and philanthropist, not because of the way he died but because of what happened when his brother tried to claim his body. According to one article, "Lindell T. Bates, son of Lindon W. Bates of New York, Vice Chairman of the American Commission for the Relief of Belgium, was arrested at Kinsale yesterday on a charge of espionage while searching for the body of his brother, Lindon W. Bates, Jr., who is believed to have perished on the *Lusitania*. Newton B. Knox, an American mining engineer, who was with Mr. Bates, was taken into custody at the same time. 'The Sergeant who made the arrests accused them of being officers of a German submarine. After being taken before a Captain they were detained at the barracks half an hour, until United States Consul Frost, at Queenstown, vouched for their innocence. Their search of the coast revealed no trace of the body of L. W. Bates, Jr.'"

Francis Bertram Jenkins, a First Class Passenger, told the harrowing story of how one woman, Mrs. Crichton, lost her life, and how he barely survived: "She was partly in the boat, I was standing with one foot on the deck of the *Lusitania* and one foot on the lifeboat, when one of the ropes broke, or the sailors loosed their hold, and the thing collapsed and went into the water. I seemed to go down a long way, and when I came up I was under the boat. It was bottom upwards. Then I saw an open port hole about two feet above me, and I clutched it but could not hold on. Then I saw a rope hanging down, which I got hold of and some twenty others too [sic] hold of it. We seemed to be sinking and some could not swim. I let go and then I saw a champagne case which I swam to but let go, and then swam for an oar. Then I saw a long piece of wood some distance ahead of me, which I swam for and in an exhausted condition reached it."

Another aspect of the tragedy that broke the hearts of many family members was the fact that so many of the bodies were never recovered, and many of those that were recovered proved unidentifiable. Albert Blicke was a passenger in First Class who was never seen again after the ship sank, and his wife, in a desperate appeal to find his body and gain some closure, circulated this description to anyone she thought might have seen him:

> "Albert Blicke
>
> Age about: 53. Height: about 5 feet 6 inches. Eyes: blue. Hair: sandy and thin. On abdomen, 2 scars from operation. Clothes: Suit, dark material. In the pocket, wallet with gold mountings containing English money and papers. Little notebooks in pockets. Watch and chain, gold and platinum. On watch is mongram, A.C.B. Ring, turquoise and two diamonds. Underwear: Linen mesh, short and drawers. Abdominal belt, silk hose, caught up with gilt clasps. Shirt marked on sleeve by monogram 'A.C.B.' and back of shirt marked 'Sulka & Co., Paris & New York.' Cuff buttons set with light blue sapphires. Collar, white turnover. Neck tie, dark. Stick pin, emeralds surrounded with diamonds."

Another terrible story surrounded Cecelia Owen and her family. On that fateful day, she was in her Second Class cabin watching her young niece, Bessie, while her brother and sister-in-law,

Alfred and Elizabeth Smith, had lunch. Her own sons, 10 year old Reginald and 6 year old Ronald, were playing on the starboard deck with her other niece, 6 year old Helen. They were supposed to return to the cabin by noon but instead came by to plead that they be allowed to continue playing. Charmed by their request, Owen granted them another half-hour of play, a decision she would regret for the rest of her life.

Just moments after the boys ran back to their game, the torpedo hit, and upon hearing the explosion, Owen took her niece Bessie in her arms and rushed upstairs to find her boys. On the way, she ran into the Smith's, who gratefully took their daughter from her and then rushed off to look for Helen. Owen continued looking for her boys and calling their names until she was picked up and forced into a lifeboat. No sooner had it been lowered than it capsized and dumped her into the ocean. A strong swimmer, she was able to make her way to another boat which was also on its side. She clung to it until she was rescued a few hours later.

Once she reached land, she was given the tragic news that she was the only member of her family to make it out alive, but then came a small piece of good news. A little girl calling herself Helen Smith was in a nearby hospital, and when Owen rushed to her, she was greeted by a child's voice crying out, "There's my auntie."

As soon as the shock began to wear off, Owen wrote her brother, Arthur, who had not come with the family on the trip: "I will try and write a few words to ease your mind & my own. You know of my dreadful trouble. I am thankful to God I am alive & no limbs are broken. My darlings are gone, also dear Alf, Bessie, Baby. Helen & myself left…I swam for my life & was picked up by some fellow pulling me on a collapsable boat (I can't spell today) I had a terrible experience. I am thankful I have my mind also limbs which are bruised all over. I am under a doctor's care and feel better than I did, but oh, my heart aches and will always. My dear boys were with me five minutes before it happened but I never saw them again…Oh Arthur, this is a dreadful blow. Everything I possess is gone and my darlings as well. Also our dear Alf and his lot…I am trying to be brave. God will still give me strength to overcome this as he saved me for some purpose.

 Your broken hearted sister.

 CE"

In the hours that followed the loss of the *Lusitania*, small vessels from up and down the coast of Liverpool poured into the area to rescue the living, but given how quickly the ship sank and the fact that the water was only about 50 degrees Fahrenheit, it was far too late for many who fell into the water and couldn't scramble onto a lifeboat or a large piece of debris. Even with the quick response, only 300 corpses were recovered, and nearly a quarter of those couldn't be identified either.

People later told stories of being picked up by every type of boat from small fishing vessels to large navy trawlers. In all, 761 people were pulled from the water, about a third of them members of the crew. This does not necessarily reflect any sort of selfishness on their part as much as it does the benefit of their experience with the sea. 94 of the 129 children on board that day drowned, not because anyone was negligent in trying to save them but because there was not enough time for the preference typically given to women and children in a disaster situation. 35 of the children lost were infants, too young to even try making it to safety.

Bjørn Christian Tørrissen's picture of a memorial marking a mass grave for *Lusitania* victims in Cobb, Ireland

Chapter 7: Certain Statements

A British recruiting poster in the wake of the disaster

A French paper's photographs of *Lusitania* survivors and victims

"Certain statements have been made which have become public, and certain allegations have been made as between the German Government and America; Notes have passed between them, and it is not inconvenient that I should tell…the statement which the United States have made as regards the requirements of their laws before the steamship Lusitania sailed for Liverpool." - Sir Edward Carson

"[A] deed for which a Hun would blush, a Turk be ashamed, and a Barbary pirate apologize." - *The Nation*

From the moment the *Lusitania* was struck by a torpedo and two explosions ripped through its hull, Germany insisted that the ship was illegally smuggling weapons from America to Britain and thus carrying "contraband of war." German spokesman Dr Bernhard Dernburg also noted that the *Lusitania* "was classed as an auxiliary cruiser," and the fact that it was in a war zone made it a justifiable target regardless of the passengers on board. Secretary of State William Jennings Bryan, who later resigned due to opposing American involvement in the war, seemingly echoed some of the Germans' positions when he suggested to President Wilson that "ships carrying contraband should be prohibited from carrying passengers … it would be like putting women and children in front of an army."

However, in its official response, Wilson's administration reacted indignantly to such allegations. A note passed on to the Germans began by reviewing the charges Germany made against the country: "Your Excellency's Note, in discussing the loss of American lives resulting from the sinking of the steamship 'Lusitania,' adverts at some length to certain information which the Imperial German Government has received with regard to the character and outfit of that vessel, and Your Excellency expresses the fear that this information has not been brought to the attention of the United States. It is stated that the *Lusitania* was undoubtedly equipped with masked guns, that she was supplied with trained gunners with special ammunition, that she was transporting troops from Canada, that she was carrying cargo not permitted under the laws of the United States to a vessel also carrying passengers, and that she was serving, in virtual effect, as an auxiliary to the naval forces of Great Britain."

From there, the letter went on to make it perfectly clear that not only were German's accusations false, they were also insulting, especially in light of the number of American lives lost and the fact that no state of war existed between the United States and Germany at the time: "Fortunately these are matters concerning which the Government of the United States is in a position to give the Imperial German Government official information. Of the facts alleged in Your Excellency's Note, if true, the Government of the United States would have been bound to take official cognizance. Performing its recognized duty as a neutral Power and enforcing its national laws, it was its duty to see to it that the *Lusitania* was not armed for offensive action, that she was not serving as a transport, that she did not carry cargo prohibited by the statutes of the United States, and that if, in fact, she was a naval vessel of Great Britain she should not receive a clearance as a merchantman. It performed that duty. It enforced its statutes with scrupulous vigilance through its regularly constituted officials, and it is able therefore to assure the Imperial German Government that it has been misinformed."

Finally, the letter hinted at actions to come. Many Americans had already been clamoring for the United States to join the war, and the loss of the *Lusitania* would set into motion a series of events that would soon see America join World War I as one of Germany's most ardent foes: "If the Imperial German Government should deem itself to be in possession of convincing evidence that the officials of the Government of the United States did not perform these duties with thoroughness, the Government of the United States sincerely hopes that it will submit that evidence for consideration. Whatever may be the contentions of the Imperial German Government regarding the carriage of contraband of war on board the *Lusitania* or regarding the explosion of that material by a torpedo, it need only be said that in the view of this Government these contentions are irrelevant to the question of the legality of the methods used by the German naval authorities in sinking the vessel."

A cartoon depicting America's disapproval over the German sinking of ships like the *Lusitania*

When America formally protested the action, German Kaiser Wilhelm II wrote his own comments in the margins of the complaint, including "utterly impertinent," "outrageous," and "this is the most insolent thing in tone and bearing that I have had to read since the Japanese note last August." However, the Kaiser also understood the diplomatic damage Germany had suffered as a result of the sinking of the *Lusitania* and placed restrictions on the naval warfare to placate the United States, at least for a time. Although Americans were understandably outraged and newspapers thunderously denounced the attack, President Wilson made clear that he still would not join the war in a speech given on May 10: "There is such a thing as a man being too proud to fight. There is such a thing as a nation being so right that it does not need to convince others by force that it is right."

Not surprisingly, the British government supported America's response, and conspiracy theories have continued to accuse the British of either instigating or at least passively allowing the loss of the *Lusitania* in order to garner international sympathy and draw the United States into the war. It's also no coincidence that the man usually accused by the conspiracy theories is Winston Churchill, who was First Lord of the Admiralty when the *Lusitania* sunk. Similar conspiracy theories have accused Churchill of knowingly withholding information about the impending Japanese attack on Pearl Harbor from the Roosevelt administration to guarantee American entry into World War II. Although he couldn't possibly have plotted the *Lusitania*'s demise, Churchill would try to make a scapegoat out of Captain Turner in the aftermath of the disaster to avoid having the tragedy tarnish the government.

Regardless of the conspiracy theories, Sir Edward Carson echoed the Americans and denied the German allegations: "May I say here, at the outset, that that being a statement of the enforcement of the Regulations under Statutes at the port of departure, New York, our evidence here fully confirms the statement that was made. There was no such outfitting of the vessel as is alleged and fancied or invented by the German Government; and your Lordship will have the fullest evidence of that from the witnesses we will call in confirmation of what was said by the United States Government."

Some would later assert that the ship was made a bigger target because it was not traveling fast enough, and this was offered as evidence that the crew was failing to do all that it could to avoid being targeted. This also played into the idea that England was setting the ship up for destruction. However, Carson had an answer for that as well, noting that "the average maximum at which she had travelled from New York was about 21 knots, and a question will arise as to whether the captain was right in travelling at the time at 18 knots. I ought, further, to mention this, because it is a matter that concerns the owners, that out of 25 boilers they had in use all through the voyage only 19…the owners of the ship, the Cunard Company, say is, that in consequence of the war and the decrease of passenger traffic between America and this country, they had determined, not merely as regards this ship, but as regards other ships engaged in the traffic, and on other voyages of this ship, to use only the 19 boilers with a view to economy, having regard to the passenger traffic which they anticipated. That enabled them to do with about three-fourths of the coal that would be ordinarily used, and enabled them to save a certain amount of labor. Whether that was right or wrong we shall probably have to inquire somewhat into. But it is right to say that even with the boiler accommodation which was in use, I understand, that the *Lusitania*, making 21 knots, would be a faster ship that any other of the large trans-Atlantic liners which convey passengers from one country to another."

There was also the matter of how the crew functioned during the emergency, as well as the state of the gear used to lower the lifeboats. Following the ship's loss, the British government held an inquiry into its sinking. It was a unique hearing when it came to investigating a sinking, as Carson pointed out: "We know in the present case that there was no accident. We know that there was a premeditated design to murder these people on board this ship by sinking her. Everything points to that perfectly clearly and perfectly plainly…The real questions that will arise upon that are only two. The first is as to the navigation of the ship, having regard to the instructions, and the suggestions and the information from the Admiralty, and the second is as to whether everything was done that possibly could be done to save human life and alleviate human suffering after the ship had been torpedoed. … There is one thing which I might state which I think all the witnesses concur in, that there was no panic. …In certain circumstances of this kind, and with the number of human beings who were on board, it is not very easy to get any very accurate description of what did really happen as regards each boat, or anything of that kind. …we shall court inquiry and evidence, as is our duty, from any other person who wishes to come forward here, and if there are complaints against either the master or the owners or the crew everybody here as I understand will have the fullest opportunity of stating it. That is one of the objects of the investigation, but as I said before, this investigation differs from all others that I know of which have been held in these wreck inquiries, because, unfortunately, the cause of the loss of life is only too clear."

The inquiry was a brief affair that lasted just five days, but during that time, the committee heard from both passengers and crewmen, all of whom agreed for the most part about why the ship sink. This led the committee to wind up its deliberations and issue a simple statement: "The Court, having carefully enquired into the circumstances of the above mentioned disaster, finds, that the loss of the said ship and lives was due to damage caused to the said ship by torpedoes fired by a submarine of German nationality whereby the ship sank. In the opinion of the Court the act was done not merely with the intention of sinking the ship, but also with the intention of destroying the lives of the people on board."

The question of whether the *Lusitania* was carrying guns or other armaments has been debated since the day the ship went down. The cargo manifest made clear that the ship was carrying rifle cartridges and empty shell casings, something the British not only admitted but conceded had been carried on the *Lusitania* throughout the war. It was only decades later that declassified documents indicated that the ship was indeed carrying over 50 tons of live ammunition from the United States to Britain. Indeed, the British government began warning divers who went to explore the wreck that there were dangerous contents down there: "Successive British governments have always maintained that there was no munitions on board the Lusitania (and that the Germans were therefore in the wrong to claim to the contrary as an excuse for sinking the ship) ... The facts are that there is a large amount of ammunition in the wreck, some of which is highly dangerous. The Treasury have decided that they must inform the salvage company of this fact in the interests of the safety of all concerned."

That said, while the Germans claimed that the secondary explosion was evidence of weaponry being hidden in the ship, explorations of the wreck have more recently led historians to believe that the secondary explosion was actually caused by an exploding boiler, not the detonation of munitions. Furthermore, it's fair to question whether the presence of the munitions truly mattered since the ship itself was not armed and posed no threat to any vessel, German or otherwise. With the possible exception of a few soldiers on leave, the ship's passengers were all civilians, so it may be better to ask whether the Germans were justified in sinking a ship full of civilians simply to keep weapons from falling into their enemies' hands. Sir Edward offered his answer, one with which most people would likely agree: "At the present moment, all I want to emphasize is that there was no warning and there was no possibility under the circumstances of making any immediate preparation to save the lives of the passengers on board. My Lord, the course adopted by the German Government was not only contrary to International law and the usages of war, but was contrary to the dictates of civilization and humanity; and to have sunk the passengers under those circumstances and under the conditions that I have stated meant in the eye, not only of our law but of every other law that I know of in civilized countries, a deliberate attempt to murder the passengers on board that ship"

A British recruitment poster that features the sinking of the *Lusitania* in the background

A British stamp that featured the *Lusitania* and asked people not to buy German goods

Mike Peel's picture of one of the *Lusitania's* propellers in Liverpool

Bibliography

Burns, Greg, *Commemoration of Death: the medals of the Lusitania murders.* (August 2012), full color bleed, 194 pages.

Bailey, Thomas A. and Paul B. Ryan. *The Lusitania Disaster: An Episode in Modern Warfare and Diplomacy* (1975)

Ballard, Robert D., & Dunmore, Spencer. (1995). *Exploring the Lusitania*. New York: Warner Books.

Layton, J. Kent (19 December 2010). *Lusitania: an illustrated biography*. Amberley Books.

Molony, Senan (2004). *Lusitania, an Irish Tragedy*. Mercier. p. 192.

O'Sullivan, Patrick. (2000). *The Lusitania: Unraveling the Mysteries*. New York: Sheridan House.

Mitch Peeke; Steven Jones, Kevin Walsh-Johnson (31 October 2002). *The Lusitania story*. Barnsley, Yorkshire: Leo Coope (Pen and Sword books).

Preston, Diana (2002). *Wilful Murder: The sinking of the Lusitania*. London: Corgi (Transworld publishers).

Ramsay, David (3 September 2001). *Lusitania Saga and Myth*. London: Chatham Publishing.

Sauder, Eric; Ken Marschall, Audrey Pearl Lawson Johnston (1 October 2009). *RMS Lusitania: The Ship and Her Record*. London: The History Press.

Sauder, Eric; Ken Marschall (December 1991). *RMS Lusitania: Triumph of the Edwardian Age*. Redondo Beach CA: Trans-Atlantic Deigns.

Lightning Source UK Ltd.
Milton Keynes UK
UKHW02f2229020818
326690UK00017B/473/P